# Realigning With God
# My Journal of My Journey

**Monique McMillian**

**Editor, Jess Moore**

## WORD FROM THE AUTHOR:

Let me first begin by saying thank you for your support. When I first began my journey with God, my original plan was to document my journey for thirty days. I soon found that a journey with God is a lifetime. A journal originally designed to be thirty days is composed of a lifetime of my challenges. This book is filled with full disclosures as I work on a stronger relationship with God. I hope this book is beneficial to you on your journey with God. You will have some good days as well as bad. There are going to be days when you want to give up and turn back to the world. There are going to be days when you give up and turn back to the world, but don't give up. My purpose for this book is to be transparent to the readers especially those that are desiring a closer walk with God. It is designed to offer encouragement in your time of need. You are going to be tested on your journey. The enemy is going to fight you harder than he has ever fought before. Please don't give up and know that you are not in this fight alone. To my children, Asia and Keith, thank you for making motherhood easy. To my loving mother, Sarah thank you for teaching me about God and always supporting me in everything I do. To my siblings thank y'all for taking care of your little sister through the years. To everyone that played an inspiring part in my life, thank you for your kind and encouraging words throughout the years. Most of all thank you God for not giving up on me a long time ago. Thank you for your love, favor, grace, mercy and forgiveness.

## *THE BEGINNING OF MANY BEGINNINGS*

The Lord is my Shepherd; I shall not want. He maketh me to lie down in green pastures: He leadeth me besides the still waters. He restoreth my soul: He leads me in the paths of righteousness for His name's sake. Yes, though I walk through the valley of the shadow of death, I will fear no evil: for thou art with me; thy rod and thy staff they comfort me. Thou preparest a table before me in the presence of my enemies: thou anoint my head with oil. My cup runneth over. Surely goodness and mercy shall follow me all the days of my life: and I will dwell in the house of the Lord forever. Psalm 23 As a child this was one of the first scriptures in the bible that was introduced to me by mother and father. As a child I never knew what these scriptures meant until I got older. Understanding the purpose of a Shepherd and his relevance to the sheep. I am a sheep, and the Lord is my Shepherd. Because a sheep is not considered a smart animal, the Shepherd must lead them away from danger. Many times, a Shepard will break his sheep leg and carry it from danger. With Him there is nothing that I shall want. With the Lord there is nothing to fear, especially evil from the enemy that the Lord prepares a table in front of you. My life will be in overflow with all the blessings that the Lord has for me. The Lord will bless my life with grace and mercy as I walk on earth. Understanding how the Lord protects us from seen and unseen danger is worthy of serving Him wholeheartedly. A spiritual walk with God is the best walk that one could ever take. This walk will be filled with curves and very few pathways. Every road will not be paved, many will be gravel and often feel like you are walking barefoot. There will be unexpected bumps in the road and more potholes than one can imagine. Things will inexpertly jump out at you which will leave you gasping for air. Some days on this walk it will feel like you are tired and ready to give up but someway and somehow you will find that little burst of energy that will allow you to walk an extra mile. Many times, we hear people stories of when they found God and decided to live for Him. We are often told about all the good times and prosperities but rarely the slip ups, mess up, backsliding, temptations, and give ups are shared. A walk with God is filled with up and downs. The enemy will also be in your company on the journey. When the enemy sees that you are trying to live right, he will strive to discourage, detour, and distract you from your mission. Trusting in God is the key because when God knows your heart he will turn your mountains into hills, your oceans into ponds and your test will become your testimony. Then you will find your walk has just become a lot more pleasant. The walk will have some beautiful days that have cool and gentle breezes. The sun will smile exactly right through the clouds as the birds sing so beautifully in the trees. The ocean waters will be so calm and bluer than the sky above. You will feel the gentle kiss of rain showering you with God's love as you follow the rainbow of God's forever presence and promises. Being in the presence of God is one of the most blessed feelings that one can ever experience. God has a way of showing us that He loves us even when we are not deserving. God loves us the same way that we love our children. When my children were young, they would ask me for candy. Because I knew candy was not healthy, I would say no. My children would beg and plead until I agreed to give them candy. That night they would have a stomachache which was caused by eating too much candy. Many times, I would hold them and rub their stomachs until they began to feel better. God treats us the same. Even though he knows something is not good for us he will allow us to have it because we could continue to beg and plead. When we later suffer the consequences of our decision instead of saying "I told you so", He nurses us through the pain. What a mighty God we serve. Finally on this journey there will be several times that you will be reminded of a story of the footstep in the sand. In this story a man asked God why is in the hardest times of his life that he saw only one set of footprints in the sand. Many times, you will see only set of footprints because during those hard and tedious times Jesus will carry you. Once you decide to take this walk, you will find that the people you thought were your friends with were undercover enemies. People that you have given your last dime to will not even give you a cup of water on a hot day. Your life will begin to feel like everyday math. God will subtract the people who tries to stagnate you to add those that going to push you into your greatness. God will divide your friends from your enemies and multiply the fruits of your harvest.

## FINDING THE FIRST PIECE OF THE MISSING PIECES

When I decided to take a walk and align with God like so many others, I thought it would be a breeze. I thought that I would instantly hear God's voice and the enemies' weapons would stop forming. Little did I know that I would hear His voice, but the weapons would form but would not prosper. As Christians we feel that we are exempted from the enemies' tricks and schemes. We think that we are invisible to bricks that will be thrown at us and dismissed from the lies that will be told. It is true that God protects His children but like all God's chosen people you still will have to face trial and tribulations. By the end of your walk, you will be like a sheep who knows his Shepherd's voice. You should have faith that you can tell a mountain to move, and it moves. You should be able heal the sick and give sight to the blind with power that God's implanted in you. This walk will not be easy but well worth it. I first started my walk back in 2003 while I was in college at Alcorn State University. Even as a young adult I felt like something was missing out of my life. I had a desire to live right even while living wrong. I wanted more in my life, and I knew the only way that I could have it was by incorporating God in my life. My journey started with going to bible study on campus. Not going to lie, the football player who I had the biggest crush went faithfully so of course seeing him and admiring him secretly was at first my reason for attending. The more I went the less I focused on my crush and started focusing on the word of God. My friends and I would go to Wesley Foundation to pray and fellowship with other students and faculty members. The same Wesley Foundation that we would lie about having money runs and keep the money. In college a money run was when you go knock on dorm doors and ask for donation to help with a specific cause. My freshman year of college I was the world's worse curser. Every word that came out of my mouth was a cuss word followed by a verb followed by another curse word. It's funny how God took someone I disliked and helped change my life in the best way. One day while in the cafe there was a girl that I really did not like. This girl literally worked my nerves and made my blood boil just with her presence. I remember sitting in the cafe telling my friends how much I disliked her and wished that she would say something to me so we could fight. She was so loud, obnoxious and clearly seeking attention from everyone in the cafe. I told my friends to listen to the cuss words that were coming out of her mouth. One of my friends looked at me jokingly saying "but Monique you cuss just like that!' Funny how I could see the beam in her eye but could not see the wood hanging out of my own eye. I remember going to the Wesley Foundation, getting in my prayer corner and asking God to take cussing away from me. Because of how I dislike that girl, I was determined not to sound anything like the one person on campus that I literally could not stand. I cannot say that I stopped cussing overnight, but it did happen quickly. God has allowed me to develop a vocabulary that easily substitute cuss words with little to no effort. I must say it was hard living for God on a college campus because in college you are surrounded by temptations, parties and lust. Lots and lots of lust. I am thankful when I finally decided to seek God that He placed people in my life with the same desire to live for Him. I don't want to give the false impression that I went to college and lived right the whole time I was there. I started college in 2001, but my walk did not begin until mid-2003. My first two years of college I became a mother of two, lived in wedlock, fought, drunk, smoked and partied boy did we party. Thursday college night, Friday which ever frat decided to throw a party in the old gym, Saturday partied with the local and Sunday night we partied with the old heads. As you can see living right was not the original plan. I was doing just what I wanted to do, when I wanted to do it, and luckily I had friends that did not mind. It was maybe after my first child that I started wanting more. I moved off campus and into a home with my kids' father. After my daughter was born, I started looking at life a little differently. I wanted to marry and raise our children in a two-parent home. After getting pregnant with our second child, I realized that marriage may be part of my plan but not his. I made the first and boldest step on my walk with God and moved out of his house and back on campus. Being a pregnant college student already with one child and walking away from their father was hard but ended up being worth it. Because I never registered for a room at the beginning of the year I had to live back and forth between a friend's room. I thank God for good friends but even more for great parents that allowed me to finish college while they took care of my babies. Moving off campus was just the first step of my spiritual walk. The second step was the desire to want to live for God. When I made up in my mind that I wanted to live for God I knew some things in my life would have to be revised. First it started with the people I was hanging around. When God saw that I was serious about living for Him changes began to happen in my friend circle. My best friend did not come back to school the next year, one of my friends decided not to live off campus, one graduated and two decided they wanted to live for God as well. God sent other individuals in my life that were also seeking Him. The more I engaged myself around people my age that were not afraid to pray openly and boldly, the more I wanted to do it too. There were many nights that my friends and I would go to the chapel steps at night and pray. Sometimes while praying some students would stop and pray with us while others walked swiftly by. I guess in their minds why pray so openly especially on campus.

## ENCOUNTERING THE HOLY SPIRIT

There was this one night that the students decided to have prayer night in the dorm lobby. This night was filled with power prayers and the Holy Spirit. I was down on the floor praying and I asked God to bless me with the gift of speaking in tongue. I heard God say, "call my name three times". When I said Jesus the third time a language began to flow from my lips that was so powerful and amazing. I thought to myself this could not be. Am I speaking in tongue? I found that tongue did not just come on demand. For some reason I thought I could speak it at the drop of a dime. Because I did not speak it when I wanted to, I thought maybe it was not real. Maybe I did not really speak in tongue that night. My tongue did come back, but it was not in just any ordinary moment. I was at a prayer service one night and the Holy Spirit was so high in the building. Someone was in there started speaking in tongue. Apparently, my spirit connected to their and my tongue language began to flow but this time longer and more powerful than the first time. Many times, I would go to the Wesley Foundation, get in my prayer corner, call God's name three times and used my gift. I must be honest I did not know what I was saying while speaking in tongues, but I knew it gave me the best feeling. Knowing that I am connecting to God on a very personal level between Him and me. My transformation was visible to everyone around me. I was becoming a new person right before my very eyes. I can remember coming home on the weekends and my family and friends looking at me differently because they knew the old me. I can't say that all the looks were a good look. Yes, there was a joke and lots of sarcasm. Many people did not understand the new me especially the versus that does not mind praying for the family. One Sunday I decided to attend my home church. While singing Amazing Grace I began to cry and openly praise God. I must be very transparent that my behavior was not the norm at my then home church. When I got home my brother asked me why I cried during Amazing Grace. I could not explain. I knew what I wanted to say, but I knew that he would not understand. He would not understand how for the first time in my life I felt the true meaning of the song. I knew I could not make him understand that it was God's grace that truly saved a wretch like me. He would not understand that I once was lost but on that Tuesday night in the student's lobby when God gave me that gift of speaking in tongues that I felt His grace all over me. Trying to explain to my brother that I was blind but when I decided to give God my life not on August 10, 1991, but that Tuesday in 2003 that I was finally able to see. Living for God was not only about praying and praising God.

I had to understand how my blessing really comes. It was about giving what God needed from me, giving my 10% faithfully and cheerfully. Paying my tithes faithfully was new to me. I was used to giving five and ten dollars here and there. Giving 10% of a check that was small and barely enough. By this time, I was now a mother of two and had an apartment. One day while at church I paid for my tithes of my tithes, which was all the money I had. I got back to my mother's house and did not have a penny to get back to school. A family member told me that if I knew I had to go back to school then why did I pay so much in tithes. I told them that was my ten percent. Funny, the very person that questioned my giving was the person that God used to bless me with a hundred dollar without my asking. I gave one hundred dollars in tithes and God gave that one hundred back that very day. It was my last year of college and like mention I had moved off campus. It was God who had me to walk out of my apartment at that very moment to meet a special neighbor. In conversation we talked about school and exchanged numbers. After a few days my neighbor invited me to attend her church. I knew it was God because I had been praying to hear a word from God. The church was small and found in the backwoods. There was so much power in that church which helped me to develop an even stronger relationship with God. My relationship with God had become so strong that literally I could hear His voice clearly. One day God woke me up out of my sleep and told me that danger was coming my way from my ex-boyfriend. I really did not understand the warning until he came beating on my door and barging into my apartment that very night. I am not going to go into deep details of the event, but God's protection was so sufficient that night. He allowed my phone to ring in another room. Did I mention it was midnight, and I had absolutely no one that would call me that time of night? I really believe in my heart that it was God calling because no one ever mention to me that they had called me that night. When God's protection is on your life the enemy himself cannot touch you. God will send His angels to build a fence around you that the enemy cannot get in and you cannot get out. Many times, I can relate to several stories in the bible. When walking with God you become a target to the enemy. When I first began me realign my relationship with God a friend told me to be careful enemy really began to attack you. I really did not completely feel that statement until I began the new walk. The enemy does everything that he can to distract you and detour you from God. When I say realign that means that I had to start over and do it again because life happens. When I left college, I found that my life had begun to change and many times not for the better. In college I had a dedicated support system that was doing and wanted the same things that I wanted. Moving home

my family and friends were more traditional Baptist and did not understand a lot of what I was feeling and going through spiritually. Lack of spiritual support will lead you in a direction that you would have never thought.
Sometimes I found myself feeling like I was in spiritual quicksand. It felt like I was sinking further and further, and no one could see me spiritually about to drown. I wanted something but could not find it. I knew what I was missing but had no idea how to get it. I was starving for a church home that was not so Baptist. Please do not think that I am speaking badly of the Baptist religion. I grew up under the Baptist denomination. One day I was sitting on my porch literally drowning in my tears and fears. A neighbor stopped by home and after a long, well-needed conversation, she invited me to her church. When I went into the church I instantly began to cry. For the first time in a long time, I felt a sense of relief. I literally cried through the whole church service. I knew at that moment

my life was missing God. Yes, I prayed and went to church but did not have that same relationship with Him. The relationship I had with God was intimate. It was better than any relationship that you can ever imagine. Just being in God's presence was better than being in the arms of any man. God and I had the type of relationship which I could clearly hear His voice. One day I found myself really stressed about some results from a test. I was driving to work, and God spoke to me and said, "worry no more your results will be in today." Surely enough I received my result, and it was just what I expected. Being in God's presence and feeling His arms wrapped around me was a feeling I continued to long for. I prayed for God to send people in my life that could help me to get where I needed to be in life. God place this incredibly special, God-fearing couple in my life. This couple pastored a small church in my hometown. I attended a few services at their church and for the first time since leaving school I got that feeling again. I went to one church service and there was a young man that brought his friend for deliverance. On that day, I saw true deliverance. The spirit was so high in the building that the preacher never got the opportunity to preach. I prayed so hard in that service that I was sick from exhaustion for three days. When the enemy sees what wonderful things are happening, he uses people to be a part of his plan. The enemy used the owner of the building to end the lease, so the church had to move. Just when I was on a spiritual high here goes the collapse. Just when God allowed me to experience my calling now the church is gone. I stayed in contact with the couple for spiritual support and boy did I need a lot of support. Lost and confused I began to sink. I allowed the enemy to use me in ways that was unpleasing to God and My temple. After struggling for many years, I finally decided to take the walk and realign myself with God. Come with me as I take my walk.

## MY JOURNAL OF MY JOURNEY

When talking to God the first thing I realize is that God already knows. Many times, we say what we think God wants to hear. We lie to others and hope that we can lie to HIM as well. We find ourselves wanting to tell God part of the story and a part of the truth. Maybe because we are ashamed of the truth or do not want to admit our sins. Developing or reestablishing a relationship with God is hard at first. When you make up in your mind that you want to live for God; the devil WILL attack. The devil will use everything and everyone to try to destroy you. The people that you thought loved you will be the very ones he uses the most. You will feel sometimes like you are in quicksand. As soon as one problem is solved three more arise. You may even find yourself questioning "is living for God worth it?" The devil will even put people in your view that life seems to be so perfect even though they are not living right. The bible tells us "Do not be fooled by the wise of the devil." In Matthew 4: Jesus was in a fast for forty days and nights and the devil came to tempt Him. The devil first tried to play mind games with Jesus by saying "If you are Son of God turn these rocks into bread". Jesus responded by saying that "for it is written that man shall not eat just bread but be filled by the word of God". You would have thought the devil would stopped there but he became bold and tried to use God's word against Him. He told Jesus to throw himself off the mountain because it is written that God will allow His angels to catch and bring Him back up. Jesus looked at Him and said " It is written again; thou shall not tempt the Lord thy God. At this point you would have thought the devil would have tucked his tail and ran but now he had one more trick up his sleeves. He took Jesus higher in the mountain and offered Him everything if He would worship him. Bold right? Offering the son of the maker and creator things that already belong to Him. Jesus just looked at him and said "It is written that thou shall not worship no other god. And told the devil to get behind Him. If the devil tried to tempt Jesus then what makes us believe we are an exception. If you do not like chocolate, then the devil will not tempt you with chocolate. Instead, he will use those that you find most desirable and to your liking. We must be smart and not fall into the devil's tricks. Building a relationship or realigning yourself with God starts with a daily plan. I had to realize that my life was falling apart right in front of my eyes. It seemed like every time I honored a dime I had to spend a dollar. I knew I had lost connection with God because it became harder for me to pray. One night I decided to write God a letter. This letter was sincere, honest and open. I knew it was no time to tell half-truth because my life was at stake. I had to be truthful not just to God but myself as well. I stopped many times while writing because I struggled with what to say. I had to speak from the heart and tell God all about it. Again, God already knew He just needed for me to say it. I encourage everyone who finds themselves struggling to pray, write God a letter. I found it easier to write what I was feeling than say it. God already knows but he is waiting on you to tell Him what you want. In James 4:2 it says we have not because we ask not. What are you needing God to do for you? What do you need from God? What do you want God to do? Is what you asking God to do a need or a want? What is your motive? Motive? Yes, what is your motive? Why are you asking God for what you are asking him for? Are you asking for a bigger bank account because you want to truly bless others and fight your way out of debt or is it for others to see how well you are doing? What is your motive? Again, developing a real relationship with God requires your honesty. I can't speak for God and say what He will and will not do. If you want a bigger bank account so you can brag, please remember James 4:16-17 tells us but now ye rejoice in your boasting: all such rejoicing is evil. Therefore, to him that knoweth to do good, and doeth not to him it is sin. Word of advice be careful! Day 1: Your letter to God: Please remembers to be open and honest. He does not want to hear your half-truths. Talk to Him! He already knows! Get to writing! God's ears are open. In this journal I will share daily routines that helped me realign with God. As a fair disclosure I am not where I need to be in Christ. I am currently in my desired mode. I am struggling to gain my relationship back with God. My biggest desire is to hear God's voice and know that it is Him. I once had that relationship with God that He literally woke me up in the middle of the night with an itchy foot to let me know that I was in danger. I remember waking up and was like "what's up God?" I talked to God like that because that the type of relationship we had. God proceeded to tell me that my caused physical to me. But God being my protector I am alive today to write this testimony. My desire again to be back in that type of relationship that I can hear His voice clearly. I hope you are ready to begin a new life, a new walk with God. Please do not think it will happen overnight. You are going to make mistakes. You are going to revert a time or two but please don't give up. Please keep fighting, fight like your life depends on it because literally it does. God is on your side. You are waiting for Him. He is waiting for you to begin your journey. Realigning your life with God is a process. Many times, we want instant results and hope everything changes overnight. Now trust me when I say some things can change happen overnight because we do know that God is a sudden and immediate God. What may be a year in our time can be seconds in God's time. Faith is the substance of things hoped for, and evidence of things not seen. The bible tells us if we have faith the size of a mustard seed that we can tell a mountain to move and it will jump in a sea. There are going to be times when it seems like your world is falling apart, bills are coming in faster than money, your children are getting in trouble, your car broken down, and your marriage or relationship is barely holding on by a string, but God is saying I am still God. God loves us. I know it's easy to pray and thank God when everything is going well. There have been times when I wanted to pray but did not believe in my own prayers anymore. I knew what God could do but the enemy had me so caught up in my situation that I lost focus on God. The enemy led me to believe that what I was going through was my fault and God did not want to hear from me. I allowed myself to go through things that God was waiting for me to bring to Him. My prayer life had gone from speaking in tongues to barely speaking to God. The enemy had me bound. Now I give the enemy no glory or credit but simply acknowledging that I allowed him in my life and space. I allowed him to steal my joy, kill my faith, and almost destroy my life BUT God! Even when I forgot who I belonged to, God sent people in my life to minister, encourage, and pray for me. When realigning with God it is vital to build spiritual relationships. These relationships are important because during your tough times you are going to need people who can intercede for you. Unfortunately, everyone will not be able to go with you on this journey. There will be family and long-term friendships that will end due to the change in you. People will not understand why your music choice has changed, why you chose not to gossip anymore or why you chose to love the people that despitefully misused you. Don't worry when people begin to be removed from your life and out of your circle. God must remove those people out your life to replace with new and beneficial ones. I think one of the hardest parts about realigning with God is losing old friendships, relationships and family. We will find that often it is not those people's real intention to hurt you. The enemy uses the ones closest to hurt us but Ephesian 6:12 says "We wrestle not against flesh and blood but against principalities, against powers, against rulers of darkness of this world, against spiritual wickedness in high places." The enemy will try to use the ones that you love the most. Developing spiritual relationships is a must. Everyone may not have a list because you may not have a church family. You may be the chosen one in your family so that spiritual support from family may not be present. Don't worry! We serve a God that knows all things. He will send the right people into your life. In your prayers ask God to send the right people your way. Philippian 1:19 says "For I know that this shall turn to my salvation through your prayers, and the supply of the spirit of Jesus Christ". Day 2: I developed a list of people who can provide spiritual support to me. Prayer is a key factor to realigning with God. As I mentioned before and will probably mention several times throughout this book, my prayer life had become very poor. I found myself offering God lazy prayers just to say I prayed. Trust me I felt the outcome of lazy prayers. God gave me the same effort that I was giving Him. When I finally got sick and tired of being sick in tired I knew it was time for a change. The first change began with how I was praying. I had to get out the bed and on my knees again. Praying in bed made me too comfortable. I wanted to say a really quick prayer so I could snuggle up in my bed and watch an old movie. Yes, I offered Jesus the bare minimum just so I can have the pleasure of saying I prayed. I had to soon revert back to when I was a child and prayed on side of my bed. As a child I did not understand the importance of bedside prayers. Even Jesus had to take out time to pray. Prayer was His landline to God. Luke 6:

12-13 tells us how Jesus prayed to God before selecting His twelve disciples. Matthew 26: 39-46 tells us how Jesus went into Gethsemane to pray when He knew it was close to Him dying on the cross. Matthew tells us how Jesus felt sorrowful and heavy because He knew that his time was drawing near. He took Peter and two other disciples with Him and told them to watch and pray. Matthew 26: 39 says that Jesus fell on His face and prayed. So like Jesus I had to get out of bed and fall on my face and pray to my Father. Once my prayers began to increase I found myself praying in my car, while exercising or anytime I was by myself. Prayer had to become a part of me again. I found comfort in the midst of praying. It seemed like whatever I was going through at that time became smaller. I had begun to find peace in the midst of my storm. God led me to begin my prayer with the Lord's Prayer. I would asked God to do whatever I needed in His name. One Sunday at church my pastor told us that Jesus's name holds all the power and whatever we asked must be asked in Jesus's name. I understand different religion calls Him Jehovah, Master, Lord, God and etc. Mark, Matthew and Luke, all tells us how Jesus went into the coast of Caesarea Philippi and asked His disciples "whom do men say that I am" after hearing all the names from the disciples Jesus asked them "But whom do you say I am". Peter answered and said, "Thou art the Christ, Son of the living God." It does not matter what we call Him if we know who He is. In John 14: 6-14, Thomas asked Jesus how we know the way. Jesus answered Thomas and said "I am the way, the truth and the life and no man comes until the Father, but by me. Philip asked Jesus to show them the Father. Jesus answered and said, "Have I not been so long with you and yet hast thou not known me" he said, "If you had seen me then you have seen the Father because I am in the Father and the Father is in me." He goes to say the magnificent work that He had done is because He goes to His Father. He finishes in verse 14 by saying, "If you ask anything in my name, I will do it." That gives me the reassurance that if I ask in Jesus's name my prayers are being heard. I had to also understand no matter how I start my prayer off the only thing that God genuinely wants me to be real when I pray. Matthew 6: 5-15 Jesus told the people when you pray don't do it just so people can see you. He says to pray in your secret closet. He says when it is done in secret, He will reward us openly. Jesus wants us to pray from the heart and not use meaningless and repetitious words. Meaning don't just say words but let your words have meaning. God already knows our heart, so we don't have to try to impress Him with fancy, long, meaningless prayers. He just wants us to speak from the heart. Matthew 6: 9-17 Jesus teaches us how to pray. He told His disciples when you pray say " Our Father which art in Heaven, hallowed be thy name; thy kingdom come; thy will be done; on earth as it is in Heaven. Give us our daily bread this day and forgive us our debt as we forgive our debtors. Lead us not into temptation; but deliver us from evil; for thine is the kingdom; power and the glory forever AMEN. I love how Jesus informs us to acknowledge God as "our Father who art in Heaven". He also tells us how He will provide the essential things to us like food. He tells us if we forgive those that trespass against us that He will forgive for trespassing against Him. We will deliver from all the temptation and evil that surround us. God has all power and glory! Tonight, I began my new way of praying Taking out time to read and understand the bible for myself has been essential. I knew I could not just rely on what I was hearing at church or from others. I must say I find enjoyment in reading and understanding God's word in my own perspective. Many times, I pray before reading and ask God to help me understand what I am reading. I often have my phone or laptop near so when

I don't understand something I simply google. Googling is nothing to be ashamed of because we are learning. In school when we had to write a paper googling became my best friend. If I can google for school, then I can google for God. The bible tells us not to lean to our own understanding. Trying not to get it wrong again is the hardest part of my journey. I think I am trying too hard too fast to be perfect and not make any mistakes. I soon had to realize mistakes are part of growth and perfection died on Calvary. I found starting my day off with inspirational words makes my day go a lot better. As I get ready for work, I simply go on YouTube and listen to morning prayers and worship. This morning, I listened to Bill Winston as he talked about God being our only source. I found revelation when he said if we have God then we are connected to everything. His message came from Matthew 14: 13-21 when Jesus's feed five thousand with two fish and five loaves of bread. Jesus looked up to heaven and connected with God before distributing the food. Because Jesus acknowledges then connect the meal went from not being enough to having leftovers. Matthew 14:20 said they did all eat and were filled and took up the fragments that remained twelve baskets full. Mathematically we will say that it is impossible to feed five thousand people with two fish and five loaves of bread. Having twelve baskets of leftovers is insane. Those insane blessings are what I am desiring God to do in my life. I want to go from not having enough to sharing and still have more enough left. I want to be like the widow in 2 King 4. When the widow's husband died and the collector came to collect, she was told if she does not make good on her debt that her two sons were going to be taken into slavery. Elisha the son of Elijah told the woman to go and borrow as many vessels as she can from friends and neighbors and bring them back to her house. Elisha offered the little oil that the woman had stored in prayer. When the woman began to pour the oil in the vessels, she had enough oil to pay off all her debts and more to store. Again, going from having not enough leftovers.

# A MORNING TESTIMONY

This morning when I checked my checking account I was in the negative. Instead of getting anxious or depressed I simply lifted my account to God and said, "God this is your account". I got dressed and went on by day like I never seen the negative balance. I was not about to allow a negative number to waive my faith. As I was driving to work, I check my email as it found that $1440 was going to be deposited in my account from my insurance company within five days. I became overjoyed but God did not stop there, by the time I got to work I received another email saying that $2100 will be deposited in my account within seven days. God could have stopped there but He did not; by the end of my workday, I was depositing $300 into that negative account. I could have easily allowed my faith to waive and let the negative account interrupt my day, but I knew the source. I know that I am connected. My goal for today is to stay connected. Ttoday~~Today~~ has been a very motivational day. Like any other day I started with my inspiring message off YouTube. The message was "There is no reason we can't have it all". The God that I serve entitles me to all that He has. I went to a patient's house and was blessed with a word from the caregiver. As a full disclosure this was my first time ever meeting the caregiver and vice versa. In the midst of discussing concerns with the patient; God's name was brought up. The caregiver told me that we are like sheep that wander into danger. She said that because of a sheep's inability to think for itself that it needs a shepherd to detour them from danger. She went on to say when a sheep insists on wandering off that the shepherd would have to break its leg and carry him to their destination. She looked at me and said many times we are those wandering sheep who can't see the danger that is ahead of us. God being our shepherd must often redirect us from going into those dangerous places. Sometimes because we are blinded by circumstances, people, situations, environment etc. God must literally break us and carry us to our safe place. I knew this message came from God to me because right now I feel like that wandering sheep. I feel like God had to break me to save me. Matthew 18:10-14 talks about the lost sheep. Jesus said " "For the Son of man ~~Man~~ is come to save that which was lost. If a man has a hundred sheep and one of them be gone astray, doth ~~he~~ does not leave the ninety-nine and goeth into the mountains and seeketh that which is gone astray. I am so thankful that God saw me wandering off and came to get me. I am so grateful that God sends people my way to offer encouragement and confirmation. On this journey I am finding myself being more open to the people that God is sending to me. It is so easy to be too busy or in a hurry and miss what God is trying to tell me. Right now, I am struggling to hear God for myself so Him sending people in path in very vital for me right now. I must slow down and listen to His instructions. In the bible when Jesus would heal, save or perform a miracle; He would give instruction on what to do next. In Matthew 8, Jesus met a man with lepers after healing the man He told him not to say no man but go to the priest and show thyself and offer him a gift that Moses commanded. Jesus gave the man clear instruction on the next step. Back story in those days any man that had lepers was considered an outcast. Only a priest can deem the person clean, so Jesus told him to go straight to the priest and offer him a gift that Moses had commanded of them. Leviticus 14 tells us the gift which was commanded was two birds alive and clean, cedarwood, scarlet and hyssop. When interacting or meeting someone we don't know if God has sent them to deliver a word, offer encouragement or confirmation so always be open to listen. Most of all be available and open to hear God's voice. Just like a sheep who knows its Master's voice, we must know it too. I admit it is so hard right now. I find myself asking is this really God or is it me that subconsciously hearing what I want to hear. John 10: 3-5 says to him the doorkeeper opens, and the sheep hears his voice; and he calls his own sheep by name and leads them out. When he brought out all his own, he goes on ahead of them, and his sheep follow him because they know his voice. But they will never follow a stranger; in fact, they will run away from him because they do not recognize a stranger's voice. I want to be the sheep who knows his master's voice. I want to get the relationship back with God that we talked like friends. When God wanted to tell me something it would always be in a strange way. If you recall me mentioning early how God cause my feet to itch bad to wake and warn me of danger.

Now the itchy feet just did not go away once He warned me. I had to ask how to get rid of the itchiness. God told me to get some alcohol and rub them together. I did and the itch instantly went away. To a baby in Christ, I know this may sound strange even unbelievable, but God's voice is real and clear. I long to hear His voice again speaking clearly to me. Tonight, my prayer is to regain the ability to hear God's voice. Today on this journey I feel stagnated. I must prepare myself to feel motivated. I am realizing the fight is not over just because I decided I wanted to live for Jesus. Today is proving I must fight harder. I can't not say it all the attacks of the enemy but also breaking habits. Just because I decided to live right does not mean my habits and desires have magically gone away. Habits are not made overnight therefore will not go away overnight. This is a process, and everything will take time, consistency and dedication. Although I felt stagnated today, I still allowed God to use me. God laid this lady on my heart that was going through with her husband. My heart went out for her when she said "Monique, I honestly don't know how to feel. I am hurt, torn and broken." I was lost for words but then God reminded of things that I have learned while on this journey. I was caution on what to say because saying the wrong thing can do more damage than good. I corrected her and said you have a feeling of hurt, lost and broken because you are not those things. Many times, when we are going through obstacles in our lives, we tend to label ourselves those problems or feelings. We used words likes I am torn, broken, confused, ugly, no good, broke and etc. Proverbs 18-21 reminds us that death and life are in the power of the tongue; and they that loves it shall eat the fruits thereof. I am being mindful of the words that I say about myself, my children, family or situation. I am even more mindful of the words that I allow others to speak over me or themselves. Finding different wording is something that I am adopting in my daily conversations. I know who I belong to; therefore, I am not in my situation. Proverb 20 says: a man's belly shall be satisfied with the fruit of his mouth and with the increase of his lips shall he be filled. Today I continue to be work on my wording and be obedient to God I am finding that temptation is real and part of this journey. I am learning not to put myself in tempting positions because I am not as strong as I would like to be. I realize who brings the most temptation in my life. If I am trying to stop gambling who tempts me more to gamble? If I struggle with fornication knowing who brings me the most temptation so I can stay out of compromising situations. Sin is all around us. I remember telling a friend about my walk with God. He told me that this is the time I must be more careful than ever because the enemy does not like what I am doing. He said the enemy is going to send people, obstacles and obstacles to make you lose focus. Matthew 26:41 says that we must watch and pray, that ye enter not into temptation: the spirit indeed is willing, but the flesh is weak. God gave us instruction to watch and pray because He knows that we are only human who struggles with the flesh. I know I must be watchful of the wisdom of the devil's trick and scheme and always stay in the word and prayer. Tonight, I will pray and ask God to keep me strong from temptations. Paying my tithes when I that bills are due tomorrow. I thought to myself if I do not go to church today then I can at least keep my tithes. God instantly brought me to Leviticus 27: 30-32 and all the tithes of the land, whether of the seed of the land, or fruit of the trees, is the Lord's; it is any of their tithes unto the Lord. Whoever would redeem must add a fifth of the value to it. Every tithe of the herd and flock-every tenth animal that passes under the Shepard's rod will be holy to God. I began to think to myself now how can I ask God for bigger blessing when I don't want to give Him the ten percent I owe. A moment of full disclosure. I have always been a tithe payer. If you ask my mother, she will say I encouraged her to pay. My finances have taken a big hit. It seems like everything that can go wrong is. During Covid, I did get out the habit of paying my tithes my thought was "why pay to a church that doors are closed". Believe me, I felt the consequences of not paying. Although I would keep the money, everything would come up to snatch it away; higher bills, car issues, food, or even lose it all together. So, trust me, I do know what will happen if I don't pay. I know paying my tithes is absolutely the right thing to do but sometimes our flesh is weak. I did not go to church this Sunday, but I did take my tithes to one of my church member's houses to pay for me. Malachi 3: 8-12 tells us if we bring our tithes to storehouse and if we do that God will open the window of heaven and pour us out blessings that we will not have room to receive. My faith is bigger than my doubt. I can honestly say I never went broke because I paid my teeth, but I have because I did not. I must be faithful in my giving

## FIGHTING THE GOSSIP

Now that I am on my journey, I honestly think I receive more calls from friends, family etc. to fill me in on the latest gossip. Yes, it is quite easy to get caught especially because gossiping was one of my habits. I know the enemy's goal is to distract me from what I am trying to do. What better way to do that than to load my ears up with what everybody is doing. I know that I cannot hear God if my ears in tied up on the phone listening to other people business. I know in this season and on this journey, God is requiring my full attention. God wants me to be ready and waiting on Him to speak. Proverb 16: 27-28 says an ungodly man diggeth up evil and his lips there is as a burning fire. A frowered man soweth strife and a whisperer separated chief friends. Proverb 17-20 goes on to say that he that hath a froward heart find in good: and he that hath perverse tongue falleth into mischief. Gossip can be consumed once a day. There have been many times that I have sat on the phone and talked for hours about other people's business. To be honest I have screenshot people's Facebook post and sent it to friends. I have played an equal part in spreading lies and gossip, but now I say no more. I want to do better than what I have been doing. I want God to be pleased with the words that come out of my mouth. Matthew 12: 36-37 says " But I say unto you, that every idle word that men shall speak, they shall give account therefore in the day of judgement for by the words thou shall be justifies and by the words thy shall be condemned. I want the words that I speak, speak for me, my character, my relationship with God. What goal for today is not listen to the gossip I got some very disturbing news today. My daughter told me that my aunt was not eating well anymore and was declining. I got incredibly sad and was feeling down because this is my mom's only living sibling. God spoke to me and said, " You said that you wanted to be a healer so go and pray for her." I was shocked and was like "What God?" Then I remembered when I was younger if someone would tell me that they were hurting or in pain. I would tell God to take their pain or hurt away and give it to me. I did not realize it then, but God was fulfilling my destiny then for now. Being somewhat in doubt, I asked God is this really you? Are you telling me to do this for real or is that my subconscious? Lord, am I ready to pray for others? What if my prayer does not work? I know it is the trick of the enemy to make me feel like I am not ready because I have not been long on my journey and not sure if I still hear God's voice clearly. I wondered if my prayer was going to be powerful enough to heal my aunt, but I do know that I had to be obedient to God. I never want to be a person that makes a mockery of God. I know I want to live for God and do his will. I am not sure if that is through interceding, preaching, or praying for those who cannot pray for themselves. All I know is I don't want my living for God to be in vain. I don't want God to deny me on judgement day because I denied Him on earth. I am reminded of Psalm 27:4 One thing have I desired of the Lord, that will I see3k after that I may dwell in the house of the Lord all the days of my life to behold the beauty of the Lord and enquire his temple. My prayer tonight is to seek my calling When realigning with God I am being to understand by the preacher use to always say be ye ready at all times. Matthew 24: 44 also say Therefore be ye ready, for the son of Man is coming at an hour you do not expect. This morning, I woke up and went to the nursing home, prayed for my aunt and helped her with breakfast. As I was praying, I began to think what if someone walks in while I am praying. What would they think? I know many would say why would you even care what people say if you are working for God. Please keep in mind that I am still finding confidence in myself and my walk with God. Again, I don't want my walk to be in vain. It is still a process that I am trying to be comfortable in. Now there is a difference between being uncomfortable and being ashamed. I am not ashamed of living for God, but I was uncomfortable knowing someone may walk in. One thing I can say about my aunt is that she was a woman of strong faith and loved me. We prayed and ministered together. I can tell that she believed in my prayer. I am so grateful that I was obedient to God. This event happened in mid 2023 unfortunately my aunt passed away February 2024. Being ready for when God send people your way is another form of being ready. Today I also received a call from an old college friend. We began talking about old times but ended up talking about business plans and opportunities. I knew this call was from God because everything he was telling I had already prayed to God about. I was encouraged to write my professional bio profile, LLC, and take professional photos which was God's way of lining me up for success. When I got home, I wrote my bio and prayed to God that He put my name in room of people that do not know me yet. I pray that God put me in room with million and billionaires who are waiting to work with me. I know it is not just my wanting to be successful but the work that I must put in to become successful. James 2:20 says Faith without works is dead. Today I will begin to put the works in Since being on this journey God has either placed someone in my path to give me an encouraging word or someone, I can give an encouraging word to. This goes back to building spiritual relationships with others. I was talking to this lady today and she was telling me about how she had planned a cruise. She said it seemed like things had begun to go wrong with the car. She when she began to wonder if she should cancel her cruise that God told her to "STOP". She said the next day that she received a call about money that may be owed to her. She said within days that she received a five hundred and one hundred dollar check in the mail. I felt blessed just to hear her testimony about how God is sending blessing out of nowhere. Just like Matthew 17: 27 when God send Peter to catch a fish from the lake and a coin in the mouth to pay the temple tax for both of them. A blessing in the midst of nowhere! Today reminded me of what type of God we ready serve. We serve a God that does unnatural, unexplainable, unimaginable miracles. As a follower of God, I know that I am entitled to the blessings of God. God has no limit in what He can do but may times we put a limit on God. We think that we are not worthy of nice things. We will find ourselves asking God for a Elantra car when we really desire a Mercedes. We ask for a mobile home when our heart really desires a brick home. We have to learn to open our mind to bigger and better things. We must know that God is doing great things in our lives. God is about to send checks in the mailbox, grants are being approved, loans are being forgiven, houses are being bought all because of our faith. Matthew 17:20 says "Because you have so little faith. truly I tell you, if you have faith as small as a mustard seed, you can say to this mountain, Move from here to there, and it will move. and nothing will be impossible for you. Hebrew 11: Faith is the substance of things hope for and evidence of things not seen. All though I can't see it right now but I know God is working things out in my favor. Tonight, I will stand on faith Knowing God is going to work it out is my mindset while on this journey. Knowing that God knows the desire of my heart. God knows if we are serious about stop sinning and if it's all an act. When we are faced in a difficult and sinful position God will change that position in a blink of an eye. Again, temptation is very real. Temptation is something that we will fight daily. James 1: 14 But every man is tempted; when he is drawn away of his own lust and enticed. When he sees that you are really trying to live right that he will send things against you. I know you have read this before, it's because the devil is continually on his job. The devil knows your weakness. He works hard to break, entice and distract us. The bible did not say that the weapons would not form. In Isaiah 54: 17 it said the weapon may form but will not prosper. I enjoy listening to the song "It's a fixed fight and I have already won". I know that if God is on my side that I have already won. Full disclosure to the enemy is at me so hard right now. I am praying hard to remain strong Today I pray for strength I am a firm believer in being honest. I feel the only way that I will be able to help others is to be 100% honest and transparent. I have not written in two days because I feel strong. I have been feeling guilty and unworthy because of my falling. I was in the place where the enemy wanted to be; feeling like a failure to God. I was feeling so guilt that I could not ask God for anything in my prayer not even forgiveness. I had to realize that God is not like man even when I fall short, He still loves me. I had to dust myself off and get back to God's business. Temptation is real but so is God. To be honest I think I had gotten too cocky and felt I was too smart to be tricked by the devil. I know this is probably not going to be the first or last mistake that I am going to make. It is my sincere prayer that even if I fall that I am strong enough to get back up and fight. I think with so many believers that we do not want to share our flaws. Many makes their journey look like it was so easy and flawless. Again, I feel that this journal is pointless if I am not 100% with God, myself and the readers. I am encouraging that may be reading this. Please do not give up. You are not a failure. It is not about how you begin but how you finish. The race is not given to the swift or the strong but to those who endure to the end. I think today is when I realize that there is no end date to my journey. It was my original idea to write only 30 days. This journey is lifetime although this journal may not be. Tonight, I learn to forgive myself I am preparing myself for a week fast. I am not sure what I want to give up for a week. I know some people eat fast food at a certain time of day. I went on a fast that I could not eat until 12pm. In all honesty I do not eat breakfast anyway so not eating or drinking until 12pm is not a huge sacrifice. I know many will have their own beliefs about fasting and what too fast. For me I want my fast to be personal; something I can give up that would be pleasing to God. I want it to be something that will cleanse me if I give it up for a week. I am going to pray about it and allow God to lead me. Personal moment: I am feeling like Peter when Jesus told him that he will deny Him three times before the cock crows three times. Peter knew he loved Jesus and denying Him just seemed crazy. When faced in an adversary situation Peter did deny God and to be honest, I know it was not intentional. He is the one disciple that I believe love Jesus more than anything. When Jesus came back from resurrection, He asked Peter if he loved him three times. I know that Jesus knew that Peter really did love Him. Jesus never gotten mad at Peter because He knew it would happen. Instead of getting mad He simply gave Peter instruction to go and teach His word. When Peter realized that he denied Jesus three times before the cock crows he felt remorseful. I can only imagine Peter thinking how I could have done this. How could I have denied the man that I love so much. I am in that current state now. I am still trying to recover from my mistake and continue my journey. I am learning to make time to pour into others. I am learning to just slow down and listen. We never know what others are really going through. I often think about when I am in store and I often speak to people about how they are doing, but I never stop long enough for them to answer. Sometimes just stopping to hear a person can be a matter of life or death. Many times, people just need to vent or just say their problem out loud. If we stop to listen that can give us the opportunity to minister and share the goodness of God. Tonight, I had the pleasure of talking to my nephew about things that he is going through. I felt so honored and humbled that he felt comfortable enough to share things with me. God used me to be a resource of comfort and encouragement to him. Life is hard, and people are going through serious trials and tribulations. It is so easy to say, " I don't have time" or " that's not my problem". What if God treated us like we do each other. What if God says, "that's your problem so figure it out". What if God turned a death ear to us and stop listening to us as we cry out to Him. Most of all what if God stopped loving us when we make mistakes. My goal is to make time to listen more I have not written in a few days. Not because I backslide or anything like that. These last few days have been "just days". When I first started writing I would write every day about my big encounters. I soon realized that there are times that we will just have days. No extraordinary moments, just an ordinary day. Deeper I get into this journey the more I am beginning to realize the plan I set are not how God wanted it. Again, I originally thought that God and I would have these big spiritual encounters every day that I would be able to journal about. I am soon finding out that many days would be "just days" Today I attended church and received an inspiring word. The preacher spoke from Job 2 about integrity. He talked about how came to God and told Him that no man loves Him completely. God told Satan about His good and faithful servant Job. God knew Job would never curse Him and even referred to him as a perfect man. Satan told God the only reason Job loves Him so is because of the riches and good life that Job has. Satan went on to even tell God that Job did not have all those things that he would curse God. God gave Satan permission to test Job but told him that he could not touch Job. Satan immediately allowed all Job's donkeys and oxen to be stolen, killed all ten of Job's children in a storm, set fire to Job's sheep. When Satan seen that his scheme was not working, he came and asked God for permission to go further. God told him that he can do anything but take Job's life. Satan instantly sent sickness to Job's body and filled it with boils and sore. Job's wife told Job to just curse God and died. Three of Job's friends came and talked about him verse 4 41. In verse 42 God blessed Job doubt for his faithfulness and integrity. The preacher ended his message by asking the congregation a question. A question that left me feeling concerned with my faith. He asked, "If God could've trusted you enough to turn Satan a loose and you not curse God?' My goal is getting where God can trust me like He did Job God continues to send people in my path to encourage and bless me. Today I received a call from an old friend who I have not talked to in months. He shared with me that he and his wife have started a church and wanted me to attend. In this conversation we talked about things such as; God's calling, my future husband, their church, family and ministry. Need I say that we were on the phone for about three hours. He asked me a question that took me by surprise. He asked if I was a prophetess. I immediately said "no". He asked me why I answered like that. I told him that I did not want the responsibility of bringing bad news to people. He kind of giggled and explained that prophetess is not about the bringing of bad news but good news to God's people. That conversation left me wondering exactly what I want to do for God. I once prophesized that I would be an intercessor. Being an intercessor just fits my desires of standing in and praying for others. I honestly feel bad for those that are going through sickness and tough times. Many times, when I am at the altar, I forget about my problems and find myself praying for others. I am learning to put myself aside and help others even when I do not feel like it. I must be ready to pray when God tells me to pray. Go when I don't feel like and be obedient to God.

THE ENEMY'S SCHEME Today the enemy tried to plant negative thoughts in my head about co-workers. I instantly began to plot how I would respond in the meeting. I told of one my co-worker that I knew that God had me covered. I boldly spoke about how God favor me and is pleased with me. I began to think about Isaiah 54:17 no weapon formed against me shall prosper and every tongue that shall arise against thee in judgement thou shalt condemn. Again, the word never says that the weapon won't form but it will not prosper. No matter what is planned against me I know God has me in a protected fence. A fence I cannot get out and the enemy cannot get in.

No matter what the enemy sends at me I know my faith is bigger than their plots and scheme. My faith is bigger than any lie that could be told to me. I walk by faith not by sight. Today I recognized and was obedient to God's voice. On my way to work today God spoke to me and told me to buy a book from this new author. I reached out to her and asked how I could buy her book. She told me about Amazon, so I did. I am not sure why God instructed me to buy this book, all I know was to be obedient. I am so thankful that I am beginning to hear His voice again. I know that I have mentioned it earlier, but I want to be like the sheep that recognizes his master's voice. I know the Lord will lead me in the path of righteousness for His name's sake. GOD TELLS ME WHO MY HUSBAND IS Two nights ago, while I was in the midst of prayer, God spoke to me and told me who my husband is. He told me when I pray to call him by name and don't just say "my husband". Every night when I pray, I would ask God to cover my husband and his family. Although I never knew he would be I still wanted to cover him. God spoke to me and said his name. Full disclosure: When God told me his name I was like "huh, God where did you dig this name up from?' I do know this young man and maybe communicated with him a few times. I never looked at him and thought I would like to date him. To be honest we are total opposites. I am more talkative, dramatic and a people's person. He on the other hand is quiet, more laid back and to himself. Again, because I am still learning to hear God's voice again, I was very doubtful because I am kind of liking someone else. My thought was if it was really God or my subconscious. Like any hard head person, I still said to my husband when I prayed because honestly, I did not feel comfortable liking someone else but calling another man's name in my prayer as my husband. This morning while listening to my daily message the preacher said when God tells us to do something it is usually something simple that takes little effort. He talked about when he and his wife wanted to buy a new home in this prestige name, God told him to point at the home. He was very doubtful because the home was out of their budget. He said being a man of faith he did what God commanded and went into the neighborhood and point at the house. That God blessed them with the home because of them. I immediately felt guilty because I knew last night what God had told me. So, I stopped the message, got down on my knees and prayed as if I was about to go to bed. I called my husband by name and asked God to bless our marriage and life ahead. Now this is truly some mustard seed type of faith because like I said we do not have any communication with each other and I kind of like someone else. I wrote the date down when God spoke this to me. October 23, 2023. This is the only date I have ever documented in this journal. I wrote it so when I am doubt that I can always look back on when He told. It would be so amazing by the time I finish this journal that we are married or engaged. We will see how this turns out. I am learning no matter how simple the instruction or how odd it may sound to be obedient to God's voice before I miss my blessing. I find myself having stupid moments. Moments when I knew if I was Job I would have probably failed miserably. God literally told me who my husband and yet I gave myself to someone else. I even told this man that we are together. Many times, I ask God to bless me with a finance blessing and I take it to the casino. Stupid moments, right? I am learning what journey really means. Journey is defined as an act of traveling from one place to another. I am literally spiritually traveling from place to place; high and lows, mountain and valleys, sin and spiritual, good and bad. I originally thought that this journey would be full of kumbaya experience and smooth sailing. Although I am much better than I used to be I am still struggling daily. I honestly think this part of the story most people leave out when they talk about their walk with God. They leave out the slip up, sin and temptations they continually wrestle with daily. You don't have to be perfect for God to love you. Colossian 3:23-24 tells us Whatever you do, work heartily, as for the Lord and not for men, knowing that from the Lord you will receive the inheritance as your reward. You are serving the Lord Christ. Having realistic expectations is something I find very important. As I mentioned many times, for some reason, I thought this process would be much easier and faster than it has been. I mean after all it's not like I am brand new to God of anything. I am several months into this journal, and I would have been further along than I am, and temptation would not still be so tempting. I realize that I am still new on this journey, and this is truly a process. I must say that I am better than I was months ago. I am at a place in my journey where I can hear God's voice now. It is not as clear and often as

I would like but I am grateful for the progress. I was at a nursing home today and one of their patients was being stubborn toward a worker. I am guessing this patient had dementia because she was difficult to be redirected. I walked up to the patient and spoke to her in a very caring manner. In a second, the patient let me walk her to the dining room. I did not notice a male worker and resident were standing watching our interaction. The male resident told me that it must be something special about me because that patient gives all the workers a hard time. The male worker added that you can see something in me. After hearing that my heart was overjoyed because it is always my desire for people to see God in me. I always try to wear a smile whenever I leave my home and be in the present of others. You never know when someone is having a bad day or just simply needs a smile. I guess the change in me may not look the way I expect but it is happening on God's timing.

# LEARNING TO GET BACK UP AGAIN

It has been a few months since I have written in my journal. To be honest I fell off track. I stopped praying for my husband due to dating someone else. This relationship only lasted a short time. I fought so hard to remain strong and faithful. Satan threw things at me so hard until it literally had worn me down. Satan made this relationship feel like it was something special and different. He came in and literally swept me off my feet. He was fun and a great cook. I must say he was my missing piece, so I thought. When we first began to date at night we would pray together. So of course, I stopped praying for my husband because it just did not feel right. It felt like everything was going right then suddenly it took a turn for the worse. I cannot explain the change and what caused it so rapidly. During this time, I did have two encounters with the man that God told me was going to be my husband. During conversation, he informed me that he was dating someone else which caused me to feel a little better about dating someone else. In the meantime, my relationship with my boyfriend had gone from talking day and night to going days without talking. It had even gotten to the point that we were not even able to talk on the phone without arguing. There were days that I had to take a deep breath before talking to him because I knew it would end up in an argument. One night as I was laying in the bed debating ending this pointless relationship God spoke to me a said "he was your distraction". I knew it was the voice of God because it explained why we went from enjoying each other to barely tolerating each other. I lay in my bed feeling ashamed. Thinking how could I have allowed myself to turn my back on God when He has not been nothing but good to me. I must mention in this period I had started working a second job because my finances had taken a turn for the worse. I still went to church but not as often as I should. I knew I was too far gone because I was not even feeling guilty anymore. BUT GOD! As I laid in the bed feeling confused, God reconfirmed to me who my husband is. I asked God for forgiveness, dust myself off and started living for Him this time full force. I would get up every morning and walk so I can spend time with God before my day get started. I looked for months for my journal to start back but I had misplaced it somewhere. One night while having a conversation with God I questioned if my husband was really my husband. (No, me and the guy are not together or even dating. He was in a relationship the last time I talked with him). God spoke to me and told me to rearrange your room. I did not understand why but I knew to be obedient. In my mind I am thinking does God want me to make space for my husband? I got up and started moving things around and right at the edge of bed was my journal. I looked in that spot before and had never seen it but this time it was there staring me in the face. As I began to look through it, I came to the dated page when God told me who my husband was. I at once went into praise because it was confirmation. Months ago, I began writing my husband letters telling him about my day and if we had any encounters. I began to stand and walk on faith. Every night my daughter and I would read the bible together. Well, I had been reading it on my own for about months. One night while she was in my bed she asked if we could read together, which turned into a nightly routine. Nights that I must work late or overnight I still pulled my bible out to read. At first, I was a little ashamed but then I thought about Luke 9:26. I began to read and talk about God more to my co-workers. On Sundays when I had to work, I would clock out and go and pay for my tithes. I was not playing around anymore. I lost focus once and promise God and myself that I would not lose focus again. One day while walking in the rain praying God enhanced my tongue! I was like "what God"! Oh My God I have been wanting this for years. I spoke in tongue but it was very few words BUT God allowed full conversation with Him in tongue. I knew God was pleased with me again. I realized realigning does not mean that I won't fall. It means when I fall, I won't stay down. I am up now fighting harder than ever and excited to me living for God and writing again. I find myself having to be patient. Each time I try to do it myself I find a way to mess it up. Example: My husband and I are still not today as of today. We have just a little more interaction than before but not much. I find myself getting so impatient with and sabotaging what could be. Full disclaimer; Knowing who your husband is and not being with him is not for the weak. There are many days I ask God "Lord why did you even tell me who he is". I find myself questioning if that was really God's voice that I heard. I would then go back and repent because I know it was God's voice. I find myself in my car preaching full sermons to myself. My message today was "wait". I began to think about how in the bible days that people relied on word of mouth. They did not have the technology that we have which could get messages across in seconds. They used word of mouth to testify about the miracles that Jesus was performing throughout the nation. When the people heard that Jesus was coming to their town they prepared and waited. They waited to see what Jesus looked like, see what type of miracles He would perform, even waited for their turn to be blessed or healed. My mind went back to the woman with the issue of blood. How she had been bleeding for twelve long years. My mind could only imagine how she felt hearing that Jesus was coming through her town. I can imagine the thoughts racing through her head knowing she may be healed. I wonder if she stayed up all night preparing to see Jesus. I see her forcing her way through the crowd trying to get in Jesus's present. I can visually see her stretching her arm, thinking if I can only just touch the hem of garment. How she had to maneuver her way through the crowd trying to get closer enough then finally getting close enough to touch Jesus. When she touched Jesus the power of her faith sent an electrocution through Jesus's body that He had to stop and ask, "Who touched me'. How all her waiting paid off when Jesus made her whole. Isaiah 40: 31 says they that wait on the Lord shall renew their strength; they shall mount up on wings like eagles; they shall run and not get weary; walk and never faith. Yes, waiting is hard. Yes, waiting is frustrating! Yes, waiting is depressing. Yes, waiting is worth it. On this journey I am learning to wait on God's timing. While on this journey I have made so many mistakes that I cannot count. I roadblocks and obstacles that were put in my path. I back slide and fall. Many times, I gave up and threw in the towel, but God threw it back and said wash your face because this fight is not over yet. I never thought I would find so much excitement in reading my bible. I find myself wanting to be alone so I can pray and thank God. Many mornings I would just sit in my car and talk to God. We talk many mornings like best friends. I try not to sugarcoat anything with God because after all He already knows my every thought. There were several times in the bible when Jesus knew what the disciples and multitude were thinking. He would usually answer their questions by using parables and not just saying "hey I can hear what you are thinking". My goal is always to be as truthful and open to God as I could be. Living for God does not mean that the enemy would stop attacking you. Many times, he will make you want to live for the world was easier. To be total honest he is only doing his job which is to steal, kill and destroy. Satan would never attack his own people. Why would he? I am remember reading when that Jesus was Satan because He was casting demons in God's name as well as forgiving people of their sins. Jesus spoke to the people and said, "a house divided will perish, why would Satan cast out his own people". When the enemy is at me so hard that lets me know that I must be doing something right. When it seems like everything that can go wrong is going wrong means God is about to bless me the enemy does not want me to have it. Many times, I feel like Job; feeling the attacks from the enemy but I know how Job story ended. God gave Job double for his suffering. I know that God is opening the floods gates of heaven and about to pour me out blessing that I can share and have plenty left. I may even go fast this week. I literally sing " I just can't give up now, I come too far from where I started from. Nobody told me the road would be easy, but I don't believe He brought me this far to leave me". Tonight, I am going to bed on fire for the Lord. Trusting God's timing is the phase that I struggle with the most. Waiting on God to do all the things that He says that He will do. As believers in Christ, we become discouraged in our waiting season; wanting things to happen when and how we want them to happen. We other questions our abilities to hear God because He has not answered that prayer yet. My father would always say that " He is an on time God'. It was not until I was an adult going through real life problem when I really understand what "On time God' really meant. My brother shared a testimony with me that really touched me to the core of my soul. He said that he had a bill that was due early the next morning. That night he laid crossed his bed and cried out to God to send someone his way because he had run out of options. When he got up, he was worried because the bill was due early that morning and things were not looking promising to him. He said before he could even ask God about the money that he received a call telling him to meet them at the bank to pick up the money. He said the person that blessed him that morning had just rejected him that night. God told him so you thought I forgot about you. You thought I did not hear you. Yes, it is hard waiting especially when you do not see a way. Yes, it hard waiting when God has given you a time that is quickly approaching but the situation still looks the same. To be very truthful as I sit here waiting for God to fulfill my husband promise to me, I get discourage. He and I still not any closer than we were when God first revealed it to me. We are worse. I have tried to but my "hurry up spin" on it as messed it up. I go so inpatient that I tried to help God out and made matters worse. I know that God is still God and His word is still His word. I am trusting God despite how it makes look today. I do know that God is an instant, sudden, immediate, right now God. Most of all I know that He is not a man and cannot lie. I told God on yesterday that I was going to reactivate my faith and start back planning my wedding. I got to have that Noah type of faith. Although it may sound crazy planning a wedding with man that you are not even in a relationship. It sounded crazy to people that Noah was building a ship. He was laughed at and mocked but when the rain began to come, and it poured for forty days, and forty-night Noah was safe and secure in the ship. I must learn to live in the spiritual, not the physical. It is important to realign with God and not spend quality time with Him. My best time with God is late in the midnight hour or in my car. This is the time that I can hear God the best because it is quiet, and everything is still. As I mention before I find excitement in reading my bible at night and understanding the word for myself. Reading the word makes me feel closer to God because I feel like I understand His journey better. It makes me feel so good when I am in a conversation with others about God and I can add my input on information that I have personally read myself. SPIRITUAL ELEVATION On tonight I completely gave myself to God and the Holy Spirit. I asked God to take me to a new level in Him. I went deeper tonight in my tongue than I ever had before. I asked God to use me as a vessel so I can pour into others. I never thought that I could love God so much. I know this elevation does not mean I will be exempted from the wisdom of the devil. This elevation means I would be equipped to handle the wisdom of the devil. This elevation does not mean that I will be free from sin. This means that I will not waddle in sin. This elevation does not mean I will be perfect. This elevation means I will strive to please God. I often find myself talking about God even in casual conversations. I noticed that I share verses and scriptures that I have personally read myself more with others. When I am sharing God's word with younger individuals, I find myself telling them in story time forms. I make it to their understanding and entertaining. I know God is preparing me for greater works. Faith! I found on my journey that faith is the wheel that keeps everything moving. Without faith it is impossible to please God. The bible says "faith is the substance of things hope for, and evidence of things not seen. Believing that something is going to happen even when everything around you are showing it is not. I am truly learning what it means to walk by faith and not by sight. I find myself walking in my spiritual and not my physical. Knowing God is working in my favor even when I am not. When the doubt and anxiety began to kick in and things are not seeming so promising I often remind myself of God's promise. Having faith is easier said than done. God knows that we are human, and it is in our nature to worry. I feel that why he picks something as small as a mustard seed and told us to have that much faith. Mustard seed type of faith is all God's requires. Believing in the impossible (well what man says impossible). We do know that all things are possible for those that trust in the Lord. God is so awesome! As I continue my journey, I am being watchful of the counterfeits. When God is closer to fulfilling His promises, the enemy gets nervous and start sending counterfeits. I feel that God is so close to uniting my husband and I because of how the enemy is acting. He has sent so many counterfeits my ways trying to distract me. Now it all makes sense. One night I got really discouraged and asked God "why did you even tell me who my husband going to be. God told me because you would have given up on him. God knew to tell me who my husband is so when the enemy began to send the counterfeits I will not be fooled. Lately, exes have been calling and trying to reunite with me. The enemy took it as far as to send the one ex-boyfriend that could keep my attention for hours. Satan knew I enjoy meaningful conversations more than anything, so he tried to send that one ex back. Unexpectedly I received a call from an unknown number and the conversation immediately began. I knew it was a set up, so I put my guards up. Like I mention earlier in the book that the enemy will try to tempt you with things that he knows you love a lot. I must say that he tried and failed. Mission not accomplished! I am waiting on my Boaz.

## THE SIGN

Many nights ago, I had begun to feel discouraged. I may have written about it not 100% sure. I asked God to send me a sign, but not just any sign. I was extremely specific with this sign. I wanted something that was unusual and out of the ordinary. Last night as I was driving home God did it. When it happened, I immediately smiled and began to thank Him, but I knew it was not anyone but God. I promised God that I would not ask Him for another sign because He did just what I asked. Now I wait for His promise to be fulfilled. I have noted how my praying method has changed since elevating on this journey. Lately I have been starting off with the Lord's Prayer which I don't recall ever doing before. I did not understand at first then the Lord drew my attention to "forgive us our debt as we forgive our debtors". God told me you cannot ask me to forgive your debts if you are still upset because a certain person never paid your money back. To be truthful I have been upset because a person asked me to borrow money and promised to give it back on a certain date. I have heard about activities this person participated in and saw items they bought but did not pay me. I contemplated if I should ask for my money several times. God then began to lay the Lord's Prayer on my heart as I pray. Now it does not bother me at all because God has replaced that money many of times. God has blessed for being obedient to Him. All my debts are forgiven I was at work and wrote my favorite scripture, Matthew 6:33 on the board. One of my co-workers asked if I had written it. I asked yes and asked if she recognized my handwriting. She said "no, it not your handwriting, you are the only person here that is so open with your religion. At first, I did not know how to feel about that. Then a warm feeling came over me. If she notices that I talk about God a lot that means I am serving my purpose. that means I talk about God more than I realized. Others are noticing that God lives in me, and I am not ashamed to talk about His goodness. Her saying that to me made me want to run on a little while longer. I felt so good that night. God has really been working things out in my favor and opening doors that I did not know could be open. I needed to stop procrastinating. God told me several months ago to go pick out my car and start making plans for my new house. I was like "God how?" God told me to just do it but because I had little faith I did not. Now months as gone and people around me are being blessed I asked God when it will be my time. He responded and said, " I have been told you to look for your new car and start making plans for your new house". God stopped me in my tracks. Above my bed is my vision board and this book is on there. I procrastinated for months before I even got serious about publishing and typing it. God told me "Faith without works is dead". Ok I hear you God time to get serious. I began to look for my new dream car. When God saw that I was working He began to release blessings. My God is good. God began to place me in opportunities that would allow me to pay off debt so I can afford the car I wanted and not just the car I can get. He told me if I give it to you, it's yours. God allowed a bank that I would not ever think in a million years to approve me for a car. I believe He allowed this bank so I can know it was Him doing the approving. Then I saw a piece of land that I wanted. Every day I would go and pray over the land and ask God to bless MY land. God allowed me to locate the man that owns the land (a man that lives in another state) and granted me favor in the eyesight of this man that he has agreed to sell the land to me. Land for me and my husband's new house.

God said just do what I tell you and leave the details up to me. When I say that God's plan is all worked out for me. I get so full and overjoyed just thinking about how much He really loves me. God told us in Habakkuk 2:2 to write your vision and make it plain. I can say that 90% of the things I have written down on vision are complete or in process. My God! My God! My God! God has really been blessing and elevating my life. On yesterday I believe God tested me to see if I was serious about doing what I asked him. So, I received a call from an individual who was in a bind. Due to my own personal reasons, I told them no I could not help them. I felt upset because of the burden that I was put on me to help. After about a few minutes I started thinking about all the things that I am asking God to do for me. I then start thinking about what kind of dent my checking account would take if I loaned the money. God spoke to me and said as clear as I could hear " what about your saving account?" I could not argue with God, so I went and got the money and loan it to the individual. So, I went to Krispy Kreme and ordered two donuts. The lady at the window thought my debit card cover was funny and blessed me with four donuts. I was so thankful and instantly started thanking God for the extra donuts. Not even one hour later I received a call asking me if I purchase a yard sign for an individual. I told them yes and was informed that the seller was trying to contact me for at least a week. I told them to ask the seller when I could pick it up and how much I owe. The person asked and the seller said today, and I owe nothing. I was like, I know this is a $65 to $100 sign, and she is giving it to me free. I was so overjoyed that I had to tell somebody. I went to thanking God because now He is really showing out. God said wait I am not finish yet. Not even one hour after that did an individual give me $40 and said it is because I am so nice and always trying to help others. My God! Three unexpected blessings in less than 3 hours.

God will reward us for our obedience. God said that you want to be put in a position to help others so help. You may not have what you want to have but I have blessed you with enough to help others. Helping others truly pays off. I am going through some of my writing material and found a letter I had wrote to God when I first started my journey over a year and half ago. While reading the letter I had to stop and start praising God. I can tell by reading the letter that I was hurt and lost. Problems and finances were weighing heavy on me. Today I can say everything that I asked God for a year and half ago He did it. I can't do anything but thank God. He had even done things that I did not ask for. Who would serve a God like this? I finally reached a comfortable place in my journey where I could open myself up completely to my daughter. I shared with her God's gift of me speaking in tongues and how He talks to me. One day I was at work, and she asked me to come outside and pray for her. I got my oil out of my car and went to pray in the parking lot. As I watched her drive off, I began to think how she believed in me. How she believes in the power of my prayer to God. I told her that I wanted others to see me the way she does. I can see the spiritual growth in her since I have been on my journey, but my goal is not just for her to grow but my whole family. I will not stop until I achieve it. I would not want to get to heaven and not see all my family and friends. It is my goal that we all make it

## AS I LOOK BACK OVER MY JOURNEY

As I read over my journal, I can literally see the growth from the beginning up to now. When I first began, I thought if I was faultless and flawless I was pleasing God. God did not expect me to be flawless or faultless just faithful. Every day I am getting more comfortable in my walk and realizing that I do not have to be perfect, just consistent. Throughout this walk I now read my bible every night, pray daily sometimes several time a day, I am more appreciative of the little things, and I share the goodness of God every chance I get. I personally think when I backslide early in my journey that it helped me to become better. When I first began, I thought I was untouchable and would slide back. After backsliding I became more realistic and gotten better equipped. I had temptation to come my way, but I was able to fight them. God revealing my husband to me is teaching me patience. This journey was full of highs and lows, good and bad, tears and smiles. I can say that every tear I shed was worth the reward I am receiving from God. When I first started this journey, my biggest concern was not being able to help God. I can say I hear God's voice and each day it gets clearer. This is the end of my journal, not the end of my journey. I am on the battlefield for the Lord. It is my hope that this journal has been a blessing to someone. If you are thinking about beginning your journey Congratulation in advance. I pray that I have written something that will be beneficial and bless you along the way. Remember the race is not given to the swift or strong but to those that endure to the end. Be blessed my friend.

## My letter to God

**This is your time to write a heartfelt letter to God. Tell him everything! He already knows just waiting to hear from you!**

_____
_____
_____
_____
_____
_____
_____
_____
_____
_____
_____
_____
_____
_____
_____
_____

_____
_____
_____

**Why is my journey important to me?**

**My spiritual support system:**

**These are people that you can call when you need an encouraging word, prayer, and/or guidance.**

1.

2.

3.

4.

5.

6.

7.

8.

9.

10.

11.

12.

13.

14.

15.

16.

17.

18.

19.

20.

**Scriptures that can help you through your darkest days.**

What's your prayer request for tonight, tomorrow and etc.?

What wording do you need to change? Life and death lies in the power of the tongue.

What's your goals for today? Stand on FAITH!


What are you trusting God to do?

Can you forgive yourself? What do you need to forgive yourself of?

## NOTES FROM THE READING

I hope you have read something that stands out and can help you on your journey!

What is stopping you from beginning your journey?

www.ingramcontent.com/pod-product-compliance
Lightning Source LLC
Chambersburg PA
CBHW070119080526
44586CB00013B/1342